Home is a Hope

Teen authors supporting LA recovery

edited by: Chiwan Choi

Qilin Press

Cover Art by Jen Hernandez
Book Design by J.W. Donley

Published by Qilin Press
Printed in the United States of America
First Edition

ISBN: 979-8-9908034-6-6

Contents

Foreword

This city raised me.

I was recently in DC for a jazz and poetry event and one of the wonderful staff at the facility said this to me about DC. That even with all the bad and the weirdness of that place, that city raised them.

And I told them that Los Angeles raised me. Actually, when people ask me where I'm from, I most often say, "LA." I wasn't born there. I was born in Seoul. The US wasn't even the first country my family immigrated to. That would be Paraguay. My first school was in Asunción, Paraguay and I attended Nuestra Señora de Perpetuo Socorro until I was in the 4th grade.

Only then did my family move to the US. Or more specifically, to Los Angeles.

But still.

That city raised me.

*

When the wonderful Frances of Qilin Press first contacted me about working together on a book to raise funds for victims of the devastating wildfires in Southern California, two seemingly opposing feelings washed over me. On one hand, I wanted to rah rah into it to help the city that has loved me as much as I have loved it. At the same time, a possibly bigger feeling—an overwhelming sense of paralysis.

We thought about contacting some of the amazing writers we are lucky to know in Southern California who might be interested. And although that sounded like it would be a fantastic anthology, it didn't really sound like the right approach for this project.

It didn't take us long to start thinking about all the young writers we work with. We've both been fortunate to have mentored and taught incredible teen writers. They are not only talented (surely beyond any level I was at that age), but beautiful human beings who aren't afraid to feel, to care, to love, to share and to celebrate each other.

As much as Los Angeles raised me and I have claimed the city as my own, Los Angeles, and the rest of the world, is theirs. It's their future. We wanted this project to be a chance for them to use their art to care for it.

*

This anthology consists of art created and donated by teen writers who answered the call without hesitation. They are from the Los Angeles area and the Bay Area and from Wisconsin and Pennsylvania. Each one sent in their work with a note wishing for the best for all the victims of the fire. The pieces, stories and poems and essays, are personal and deep and so very human.

And they all want to help raise the Palisades and Altadena and everywhere else affected around Southern California the way their own cities are raising them.

Chiwan

Home is a Hope

Teen authors supporting LA recovery

arētē

by Leah An

because it is where i reside
a paper cave i breathe the dust
the mortal's view no larger than a skipping stone
hung from the divine intervention
of insect wings.

the golden hum of a greek tragedy
in a library of tortured senses
flimsy uncontrollable thing.

and god i loved to hear her breathe
the intoxicated doctrines
of the noblest deaths
under plato's law

the spiral bound fingers
nine hands in the cave
there was no light. 37 others
the flesh of the concrete moment

a nickel a water.

We Lived Happily During the End of the World

by Pippa Barlow

After 'We Lived Happily during the War' by Ilya Kaminsky

We lived happily during the end of the world.

As the wet fire whipped outside the window.
We sat, our hearts turned cold and empty.

While they ran,
their biting footsteps on the pavement,
we danced,
Loud music shutters, its smooth sound blocking their cries for help.
Their final breaths were swatted away.
Their candles smothered by our mindless ignorance.

We were silent during the end of the world.

Our thoughts whispering inside our cavernous mouths.
Locked tight behind our jaws.

We turned blind under no threat,
And watched them from a safe distance.
We turned deaf when asked politely,
And heard the shouts of those gagged.

We were happy during the end of the world.

Grieving what we could have done yesterday, as we do nothing today.
Allowing and accepting the fate for the affected.

It was simple.
To live lives outside of the world's pain, to move on.
The shouts a constant white noise,
our simple problems rose above, pushing down all else.
It slipped our minds to sign our names in promised pledge.

Our names,
reflected back in history books.
For dissection of why we could do such a thing.
We ask why they did such a thing.
Knowing what was happening to them? People just like us?
"How could you stand idly by?" we ask unmoving.

They shout and scream, melting against our window.
The glass, a canvas, covered in blood.
We pulled in the curtains to cover it up.
In doing so,
the blood got on our hands.
So, we wore gloves.

Tidekeeping

by Michelle Bi

---

i.
and your skin tints copper under July sun as you tread
into the waves, and so what can I do but follow.
There you stand in the shallows, even though you have always
been a swimmer. In one arcing moment you could leave
the whole world behind, slip into the deepwater. You
never took an art class but you taught yourself to freeze-stop
Life. in motion and then not. the twitch of a hand or a flashing
smile flattened radiant on paper. The way time coexists as an
ocean and some infinite number of droplets, do you get it?
you've asked me before, and i never do, i still don't.
There is no paper at the beach so instead you trace fingerprints
through the sand and your fingerprints become divots and the divots
become some image of me. And even today i have some image
of you etched into my eyelids. and I still don't get it, the
in motion and not, the lines that start to wrinkle my cheeks as we
move past the dock. i confess to you how afraid i am when the water
begins to rise. But you have always been a strong swimmer
and you've captured my likeness in the sand—and of course
the passing of time is simply an immeasurable cascade
of waterdrops, which roll down your shoulders one by one as
you stand laughing, which dew at your fingertips. Draw me again,
please, before this all evaporates. take me for nothing but eighteen
brushstrokes. we are so old now and i'm afraid that growing up
is nothing but swimming into deepwater, that deepwater is nothing
but a coalescence of goodbyes, in motion and then

ii.
In other words I always return to the shoreline. Salt
stings the corners of my mouth. We have found homes
on opposite coasts and in other words I spend oceans
wishing away the distances in between. The drying folds
on my hands. Around us the tides billow and bloom
in ceaseless milliseconds. I miss something like
the shallows, like sand under fingernails

moving on (leaving behind)

by annie bryant

---

oak pollen yellow lines the crescent of my nail, grass blades brush long
    fingers against my
scarred knees, the sour scent of tarweed seeps into my skin—
the past is tapping at my bones.

how do you know when it has sunk too deep?

(there's a sparrow caught in my ribcage, there's a
       wind chime resonating in my skull, there's a
            grapevine fusing to my femur, there's a
                 memory crashing in my knuckles)

don't you remember? they ask.
what is there to remember? (or so i reply)

watching filaree unfurl after a march rain, the sight of pines dusted
    white, the slick-smooth river
stones against our bare feet, a lone coyote calling into the night, wheel-
    barrow ice melting
between chapped fingers, the quiet stillness of a morning suspended
    in frost (or so i mean)

there's something exceptional, isn't there? in the weight of familiarity,
    how a home slips into the
bloodstream, that lingering sense of solace.

peel my fist open, pry my fingers apart, and you'll see it:
dust caked in the creases of my palm.

don't you remember?
god, I could never forget.

the closer we are to fire, the brighter we burn

by Navya Chitlur

---

our bodies are made of fire // we bottle greed in our palms and pretend we do not thrive in our selfishness, and we ignore how the same drive will kill us eventually // i am watching the sun fall to the floor in california where homes are disappearing into smoke in la and / how do we exist in this air knowing we will always lose everything we build / and how do we exist knowing we continue to build anyway // tell me how to define regeneration when everything is burning / how to recognize the loss of a past when we have nothing more to hold onto // in the end our lives all amount to dust / so how can i keep holding on to my footprints on my homeland where all of my body was lost to invisible flame / and i lit myself on fire so my hand could be the one to guide my fate // our bodies are made of fire / and our birth is the first step to our predestined nature of self-destruction / so on shorelines and mowed grass / i hold my body upright and ask the oceans and fires / if they ever loved me enough to swallow me whole //

Color of Ash

by Lila Coen

I'm trying to find the words to describe the color of ash
I think it is brown like firewood like that deep blackish brown like
The space in between the cracks in between my reflection in
The downstairs bathroom mirror the one with the
Chalky blue wallpaper that rubs onto my fingertips when i touch it
I couldn't tell you why i touch the walls sometimes and i hate the
texture it is popcorny and is somehow relates to sand but i like the oil
residue left over from when he stood with one arm around me and
one hand pressed against the wall for balance standing almost into the
mirror and i was taking pictures of us as if i would forget this moment
He stands like guys do in 80s rom coms when they want to impress
that giggling girl with cherry slushy red lipstick and bows at the end of
her double dutch braids blonde hair and in a perfect world
He is still there and engraved in my hippocampus sometimes i still see
him standing like that behind me trying to take photos
I will always deny it but i was terrified he would look down and get
disgusted by the fat under my chin reflected from the bowl of the sink
and i am so so sorry–

I take it all back. Ash is orange it is the color of burnt oxygen and
burning sky red and yellow and some kind gasping under my breath
because *this is all the air you will ever have why dont you get that*

"What is the best way to die?" she asks me and digs her hot pink gel
nails into her palms. Her eyes aren't red anymore, more a dull pink
so when people ask they believe her when she says it just a cold. The
texture of her sweater looks like it was silk that someone put in a waffle

maker. Like it was supposed to be white but it was left in the waffle maker for too long and now it is some kind of orange. The sweater doesn't go very far below her ribcage. She has her arms around her knees and hides her stomach which sags when she is sitting down.

What is the best way to die? What I didn't tell her at that moment is that I need it to hurt. Because otherwise I probably wouldn't notice it was happening and I want to remember the intervals in between my wheezing for air so I can capture the moment in my head between when I stop trying and when I stop living.

What I didn't tell her is that i have come to the conclusion that drowning and melting is the same because in both cases you are trying to breathe and it doesn't work. I am so sorry i can't tell you why.

I am so so sorry my fingertips smell like asphalt when he holds them to his cheeks and tell me he misses me and I can silently mourn my wish for I wish it was last year again and the last time i have seen him is last April (2024) and that hurts Sandcastles in sand paper and I wonder what it feels like to get sand under my bathing suit when I am suddenly nine years old again and it is all okay because it was all okay

Farmers' Market

by Shyla Corona

Five, six, seven, eight ladybugs on our walk to wonderland. Sunlight illuminates the wares of my community as the white tower tents come into my sights. I peer across the seemingly endless rows of canopy, trying to spot my favorite booths. My dad tries peculiar foods while I indulge in assorted fruit from our favorite farm. He haggles with vendors in Spanish as I look on, trying to grasp at the bits of information my no-sabo tongue can catch. Another man joins in on my father's haggling. His child waits by his side. We stare at each other before looking back, standing together in our complete silence and lack of understanding. But it isn't a lonely silence. The market does not let you feel lonely, it speaks to you through the colors of posters and illustrations of heritage on articles of clothing. It sings you songs through the cacophony of voices, melding of languages, and frying of food. It seduces your senses leaving you with no choice but to mingle and create a basket of community that is entirely your own. And yet, not solely belonging to you because the market does not let any part of itself belong to one singular person. Instead, it lends you a hand in your times of isolation so that you might one day help others find their baskets as well.

As I carry my basket back, my dad hands me a strawberry made of fabric. Its vivid red reminds me of my own sun kissed cheeks. The strawberry scratches me as I hold it against my face. My dad laughs while peering down at me from his alpine station. He makes the trek down the mountain of space between my head and his own, taking the strawberry into his hands. It ascends to the height of a cloud as he pokes and prods at the leaves. I tilt my head a full ninety degrees, but the sun's rays become violent, turning my glasses into a magnifying glass of pain. A haze of dots cover my vision as my hands frantically dispel the sun's rage. When I finally gain the courage to face the sun again, a blanket of red cascades gently over my eyes. I reach my hands up into this curious fiber, trying to find the origins of its arrival. I start my search with resolution, but my hands are too young to grasp both ends of the immense folds. My dad rescues me from the confusion of my expedition as he delivers the origin into my waiting palms. Into them, he places two wrinkled straps. They hold up the expanse of textile fascinating my eyes, with its strawberry pattern and deceptive exterior.

We continue down the canopy path while I stuff the fabric back into its strawberry corner. I become a circus master, wrangling the fearsome edges into the depths of their cage. Upon his arrival to my circus, my dad forces me to free the fiber from its captivity. He places my favorite food inside, espresso almond butter. It weighs down the bag in its crystalline vessel, the first of its kind I've carried in my arms. I take time to adjust to the burden of responsibility. While passing sharp edges and nosy beasts of wonder, I cradle the bag close to my chest. My form mirrors my father's arms. I have memorized them well, growing up in the safety of their warm embrace. As the impenetrable fortress of my frame moves through the market, my father acquires more responsibilities. He does not allow me to take on more. He does not reveal the weight of these burdens in his stance or face. Yet, I see their influence in the vivid red hue moving across his arms. I hear their heaviness in the labored breaths he takes while walking. I beg once more to alleviate his struggle. He simply replies, "You are not a grown up." I am devastated to learn that I must leave him to struggle. I am devastated to learn that all adults must struggle.

He hands me an orange to remove the furrow from my brow. I place it into my strawberry bag and it keeps the butter company. The bag swings back and forth in my hand as the wind carries music into my ears. I abandon the safety of my dad's side for an audition to the dancing stage. Generations of people embrace the company of strangers in this unconventional crowd. They spin around on the asphalt parking lot, tracing the white lines of the basketball court with their feet. The woman to my right is unpredictable, moving her body in harmony with the notes of her choice. She raises her arms above her head, exchanging her joy with the sun for the warmth of its rays. She reaches for the ground, inviting a dandelion to join in her celebration. Her dancing seems to occupy a world of its own, a bubble of euphoria sustained by the band on their makeshift stage. She notices my curious gaze and pulls me into this daydream. I mimic her movements and eventually find a flow of my own. It captivates my limbs, pulling them every which way while bringing me under the surface of the melody. In the rich piano chords I learn the dreams of the pianist. In the energetic strums, I hear the guitarist's ambition. We dancers become tethered to one another within the lines of music. The rhythms, outward manifestations of the messages delivered to us in song.

My dad pulls me away from the asphalt camaraderie and leads me to a purple tent. A treasure trove of art supplies lay waiting inside. I rush over to the pocket-sized chairs and grab a canvas. While my dad talks to the town historian, I begin to record my own history. I paint the walk to this market, dotting each ladybug with exactly six spots. The humus spilled on my shirt earns a place as I look down to get the shadows just right. Philip, the apple man, carves a large apple owl for my favorite birch tree. Under that purple canopy, I call upon the skilled painters of the Baroque period to retell my tragedies and triumphs. My strokes are broad and disorganized, splashing onto my dad's jeans. He takes my blunder as a sign that it's nap time. Before we bid the booth farewell, he makes me sign the painting. I stall for time by writing my full three names, each letter in a poor scrawl of pretend cursive. Underneath my profoundly atrocious signature, my dad adds the date. He slants the numbers, giving them a chance to flee the page. When I ask why, he tells me that he does not control his writing or the pace at which years pass him by. He tells me, "You'll understand when you're older."

We begin our journey back to the car, carrying our responsibilities in bags and waving goodbye to our friends. It is noon and the market begins to pack itself up. Strawberries wandering back into white moving vans, baked goods jumping into straw baskets, fresh juice nestling itself into coolers. The band instruments dusting dandelion fluff off their strings and zipping up their cases. Our car leaves the parking lot and I watch as my traveling community brings their magic elsewhere for the day. The Farmer's Market high soothes my nerves and carries me off to a peaceful sleep.

From Downey to Anaheim, Cerritos to Torrance, the market and my father remain the only constants in my life. My mom would tell me, "Home is where I am." But she never made room for me in her heart. Her house was cold and unforgiving, filled with rage and self-loathing. Saturdays have always been a highlight of my week, a respite from the difficulties of real life. The market teaches me kindness, facilitating connection wherever I go. It is a place of wonder and intrigue, mystery, and new experience. They wait for me in each city, providing familiarity in the complete unknown. It takes a village to raise a child, and I was raised by many. The Cerritos oil man, and his gifts for me, the almond butter woman next to Chapman University, Philip, and his art of apple animals. Farmer's markets are the beating heart of California, and every one of them feels a bit like home.

Junk Shelf

by Chloe Crawford

I remember dull nights in the old house, my
mom took a step, and the walls would creak.
I remember the easiness of the kitchen sink,
metal handles on the faucet and brown
knobs on all the cabinets. I remember stiff windowsills
and painting pictures in the collected dust.

Smells of old church hymns lingered by the black fireplace.
Cousins carried gardens of jokes and innocent laughter.
Aged whipped cream cans
in our fridge consisted of our only sugar. After they left,
my brother tucked gameboards away in the hallway closet.
It remembered a child's cough and
held shrunken napkins of tears.
Punishments included scrubbing the
sticky Neosporin ground into its shelves.

Now, the hallways are white.
The wall where it once perched filled in and
there are no mistakes in
the paint, no skinned knees.
We don't risk falling anymore now
that our backyard is pavement.

the eaton fire burned bright

by Miriam Davidson

for two days, the news talk
about the day
after tomorrow. the news has not stopped since
i wrote that. the forest burns, bathing this city in unease,
coating our narrowing throats. i have never
been brave and i am not now; the sky is angry. i am not less angry
but i am less sad, like i have lost something
that was never quite there in the first place.

because there's always irony in truth.
more concerned with sending rockets to the moon
than protecting all the beauty that's right
in front of us.

the eaton canyon fire burned bright and fast.
my friends have left town. i am alone in a town
named after a rock; the city is ablaze
politicians mutter and I wonder if it is arson.
i lie on the couch and remember the feeling of
being safe. mother nature turns over in her sleep
knowing this is not her fault. this is burning the old year
—and the new. smoke fills my lungs. i am still in the living room.

as the world ends, let's listen to jazz;
spotify has a crude sense of humor.
my coffee has gone cold, which is ironic
because for two days, the news talks and the days
burn up.

Reborn

by Bella Giammalvo

Dockwheiler night
I am reborn
Birthed by pearls of ocean foam
Laying on my back
Rocked by black waves
That explode in stars
Salty against my tongue
Chapped lips burned by beer
and fire kisses in dark water
That pulls me back and forth
Deeper towards the crash
Where sky crushes ocean
Into symphony
Whispering songs in a language i have forgotten
So I close my eyes
And submerge my ears
The whole world is black and breathing

When I Think of Home

by Joshua Granados

Dedicated to the families who lost their homes in Palisades and Altadena

When I think of home, I think of warm shelter, comfort, foundation,
and love.
I think of laughter and tears, and prayers from above.

I think of memories and count to ten,
hide and seek or let it all go.

I think of squeaky doors and hardwood floors
and lines on walls that show our growth.

When I think of home, I smell French toast and bacon, spaghetti and
bread, jerk chicken, peas and rice, and carne with dad's special spice.

All eaten around the big brown table.

Meant for food and homework, hard talks, and I declare war.
Meant for grace, loud debates, and someone is always keeping score.

It's made of solid oak, scratched and weathered.
Mom insists it must stay in our family forever.

So, when I think of home,
I think of oak roots that don't roam.

They just dig deeper into the ground.
And then one day they rise up. Lost, but now they are found.

They break through the sidewalk and make the perfect ramp for a
bike jump or a quarter pipe for the black kid who skates and listens to
rap and punk.

The roots touch a neighborhood filled with generations to be seen.
Black people in houses. Our descendants' wildest dreams!

When I think of home, I think of me.
It's the place where I can breathe.

Things I Didn't Know I Loved

by Honor Giardini

---

after Nazim Hikmet

I am most alive in love. I didn't know I loved poetry until I met my girlfriend - in that I mean I love poetry like I love my girlfriend, the same way. I didn't know I loved being eleven until I was no longer eleven. I didn't know I loved reflections. I didn't know I loved allegory, and not saying what I mean. I didn't know I loved the tenderness of handwriting. I didn't know I loved LA, or walking alone. I didn't know I loved the strangers I see every day. I didn't know I loved sign language. I didn't know I loved faces that look like other faces. Walking I hear a small child mimicking another child. I didn't know I loved the lights off loved coming back. I didn't know I loved stating the obvious, maybe I did. I didn't know I love cottage cheese, or childhood friends. I didn't know I loved building-didn't know it till I had a hammer and was awful at it and bult a birdhouse I didn't know I loved endings. I didn't know I loved endings and beginnings, I didn't know I loved circles, loved academic papers, I liked lining up moments like rocks, didn't know I love small rebellions. Didn't know I loved to smirk. I didn't know I loved forks, and restaurants, and car drives, and going wherever I want to go. I didn't know I loved spoons. I didn't know I loved water, being clean, I didn't know I loved last minute projects, my reflection in windows. I didn't know I loved small victories: first kisses, dusty guest bedrooms, and dorky big eyed tall-legged girls. I didn't know I loved nervousness that can't hide itself. I didn't know I loved big rooms filled with people that make them feel small, like in first grade Ms. Fushich ran around the classroom capturing the hummingbird, when she did, we all cheered, the class walked outside and looked at its delicate body, the moment of release. I love when the speakers break and the music gets louder. I love I didn't know I loved joy until I played it. I didn't know I loved its neck. I didn't know I loved X not until I was in a room of people who also loved X. I didn't know I loved: my pants, funerals, paper, homework, gone, here, being read to. Years after childhood, M read a book aloud and I heard her and my mom together making a chord. I didn't know I loved chords, not until I counted them out. Didn't know I loved the tips of icebergs, massive oak trees with gnarly limbs, hills that look like sheets mid-shake, telephone lines, I counted them out. I didn't know I loved the chair covered in dog hair the sound of my feet, the tadpoles, and childhood enemies all grown up. what about it now that sitting on a couch thinking about your train Nazim when I'm 60, I'll love even more, I'll know all the things I didn't know I loved.

Further into the Sun

by Rasheedat Ibrahim

---

small gold hoops
on my ears, under
the black hair that
melts over
my shoulders, shimmer
like the ocean on myrtle beach
under a sunset, a sunset like
the one slowly
fading away while I'm in a Wing-
stop I'm not supposed to
be in, with people I feel
I shouldn't be with,
after walking an hour
to get there in my jet black
leggings, wearing a hat that
isn't mine, that reminds me
of the sweatshirt that
isn't mine,
that I haven't touched
in a while, gotten from
the guy we'd laugh at,
and—

Five

by Milla Jans

My five-year-old self writes that she is writing after using the bathroom. She's playing with her one-year-old baby sister, but she can't say anything except for a few incomprehensible words. I wonder what my first word was as well as my sister's, but I realize our parents never told us, or maybe we just never asked. Her sister has chubby cheeks and little tufts of hair growing from her head. She wants to feed her yogurt bites and cereal so she can enjoy the same flavors she does, but her mom says she's too young. It's unclear whether her mom means she is too young to care for someone like that, or that her sister is too young to be fed those crunchy snacks. Somehow, it can't be the first, because she already cares for someone she doesn't even know. Not much has changed. Her days are spent like this: walking around the house, looking at her baby sister, and scribbling in her diary. It's pink and purple, her favorite colors, and has an obnoxious 3-D heart in the middle, with little jewel stickers sprinkled around it. It's perfect. Her mom visits one of her neighborhood friends, and she meets her son. He's the same height as her, and they go to his room because being a girl and a boy doesn't matter at all at five years old, and he shows her his favorite stuffed dog. It's easy, somehow, even with her limited words. She also has a stuffed dog named Sunny, and it feels nice that someone understands the inexplicable feeling she'd get if she ever lost her. They hold their stuffed animals so gently, the way I hold the memories of him now. She admits that she cries when she doesn't get what she wants, and I want to tell her there is no point since she will never play with those dolls again. She constantly wants to wear the purple and black frilly dress that makes her feel like a princess. At this point, she is unsure what it means to be a princess, only that they wear pretty outfits in different colors: Cinderella blue, Belle yellow, and Sleeping Beauty pink. She starts kindergarten in September. She doesn't know what that means either. And even though she has not yet learned the word for 'hope,' she hopes she will find someone to share the experience with her. She doesn't realize she is wishing, but she is and still does.

the forgetting

by Semi Jung

---

downstairs, my ninety-year-old demented grandfather is telling my mother over the phone to *forget*.

i don't know what exactly he means by this—to forget about how he lies, drowning, in a sea of white noise all day? to forget about his white-canvas memory, about the world of his that starts and ends on the opposite sides of the white hospital ward ceiling?

forget. 잊어라. 다 잊어라. *forget it all.*

forgetting is the saddest word in the dictionary because it is human(e)ly impossible. it is a hopeless attempt to defy the unbudging constraints of humanity that leaves both the one who makes the request and the one who receives it hugging their shattered hearts to their chests.

i wish we didn't have to forget. i wish so badly that instead of forgetting, we could simply mend what has happened, drape a curtain of white over the mess and lift it to a clean surface, put the ugly pieces together and hope that they'll stay. like how i'll wake up in the middle of the night and swathe my nightmare in the layers of a bright blue dress, coat its face in the palest powder and reddest shade of lipstick i can find until it is beautiful, until the protagonist of my dreams breaks out of the darkness, until she flings off the arms of her abductor and runs away, until someone arrives in time to save her from the fire's forked tongue.

but lately i've been thinking.
i've been thinking about how most of my dreams seem to start off happily, even the nightmares. and how do you even begin to say that maybe *all* dreams are nightmares, that the good dreams are just the ones that haven't reached their turning point before your pupils meet day?

My Soil

by Jiyoo Kim-Jung

My soulmate is a place. A place which grounds my feet into the soil and shackles them to the roots of the trees I remember so well. My soulmate is a place. An oasis in a desert of withered grass and writhing plans. When my mother dragged me away from my home and sliced the ropes tying me down, mistaken in her belief that she'd give me freedom, I had never felt so light. I had never felt like I weighed nothing and meant nothing and was nothing until I was airborne in the sky, away from the love of my life. Fifty years have gone and my tender feet are back on the soul of the soil. The dirt is tender and moist, with a scent like blood if blood wasn't made from iron. The strings around my feet are short, their length sucked away as I grew and outgrew. My other half is lifeless on the ground, the roots having shriveled and withered and turned to dust while I was away, their remains still grotesquely visible within the circles of the chains. My soulmate is a place, and my heart throbs as I hear its silence. Noise indicates something salvageable, a lull indicates an end. It is an oasis that has dried, which means it is a desert, because even the desert used to be a forest before it crumbled into the sand it is now.

A Streak of Him Across the Sky

by Hana Lang

We climbed through the chipped
white paint and through the creaking
frame of the window to reach

the top of the world:
the air fresh and teasing,
while our hands pressed together.

And the night, and the cold,
and the coldness buried beneath
my clothes. We huddled for warmth.

And the black blanket tucked
the sky in brimmed with a blue
and the stars stared at me,
the white stars— at me.
And with warm eyes too—

I could feel the blood
moving in my cold fingers.

That shooting star so
big and bright and bold,
I could almost hear it—
crackle and burn and bubble.
I could almost feel it—
the warmth of his smile
across my cold starry face.

I have never met Paul before,
but when I see the many
eyes in the sky I can't help
but think he and the others
look down to find me
and to wave hi.

And we sat there, on Orleans St,
cold, on top of Her House.
our hands pressed together
while our glossy pairs of eyes—
waiting to catch one of his
streaks of a smile across the sky.

spica is the brightest object in the constellation of Virgo

by Basil Lee

Driving to
the Moon
past due
but on cue.
closer up the sky doesn't look so blue
if you could see it too
I wished on a new
                    ly born star that soon
I would come home from the craters and the dust that don't look too
different from a construction site down on earth.

Do   you
wish to
walk up here?

I wouldn't.

Stay where you
are, don't move
I'll be down soon
enough to
see you

grow up.

I've picked out a flower for you.
I hope you   think of me up here if you

ever walk past bou
      quets on the street we used
as a shortcut.

Does it feel like a long walk now? Or is it quicker to
stroll in silence knowing I'm under a different moon?

When I get back my clothes will be outdated and I won't know how to
talk to you.

Maybe you
      have coined a new way to
say I love you.

A Family Cookbook

by Emily Liu

Chapter 3, Page 14 — The Art of Folding Zongzi

Ingredients:

- *4 ½ cups glutinous rice, soaked overnight and drained*
- *1 lb pork belly, marinated in soy sauce, rice wine, and sugar*
- *1 ¾ cups dried chestnuts, rehydrated*
- *½ cup dried shrimp, soaked*
- *5 salted duck egg yolks*
- *1 bunch bamboo leaves, softened in water*
- *Kitchen twine, long enough to tie the past to the present*

The women in my family fold rice the way we fold our grief—delicately, carefully, as if the weight of our hands could tear it apart. We twist bamboo leaves like we twist memory, wrapping them tight so nothing spills out. When life unravels and the past feels too heavy to bear, we gather around the table. We busy our hands with zongzi.

This is how we stay whole. This is how we remember.

To Nǎinai, who always started with the leaves.

The first time I watched you fold zongzi, your hands moved with the certainty of someone who has folded and refolded the same recipe in her dreams.

"You must be gentle," you said, "but firm—like raising a child." You laughed then, the sound carrying a sorrow I didn't yet understand. Now, that same laugh lingers in my memory, like steam rising from the pot. The rice smelled of soy and sesame, but what stays with me most is the way your fingers trembled, just for a moment.

How to Fold Zongzi, According to Năinai

1.   Start with the bamboo leaves.

Hold them under the tap, washing away years of dust and stories. Your hands will ache, but that's how you know you're doing it right. Lay the leaves out one by one. Each leaf carries the weight of what was left behind—the part of China I never saw, except in Năinai's stories.

2.   Take a handful of rice.

Cup it in your palm as though you're holding time itself. Just enough to fill the center—not too tight, or it won't cook through; not too loose, or it'll fall apart. "Balance is everything," Năinai said, showing me the pyramid shape, held together by the softest things.

3.   Add the pork belly.

Fat marbled through the meat, tender from hours of marinating in soy sauce, ginger, and garlic—flavors that taste like home, though not the home I know. Năinai said this was how her mother taught her, and her mother before that. Place each piece of pork with care, as if it could restore what was lost.

4.   Don't forget the chestnuts and the salted duck egg yolk.

The chestnuts, soaked and softened, are little pockets of sweetness, and the yolk, golden and rich, is a sun hidden at the heart of the rice. These are the treasures of our past, buried deep so they are never forgotten.

5.   Fold the leaves.

Wrap them around the rice, carefully, so they don't tear. Twist and bend until they hold everything—rice, pork, history—tucked safely inside. Nǎinai made it look easy, but her eyes told a different story. "This is how we keep what matters safe," she said, "even when the world splits open."

6.   Tie it with twine.

Knot it as though tying the past to the present. Pull tight, but not too tight—there needs to be room for the rice to grow. If the twine breaks, so does the zongzi. Nǎinai's hands moved quickly, tying knots like sealing secrets.

7.   Boil and wait.

Drop the zongzi into the pot. The water will boil over, spilling like the stories we never speak aloud. "Patience," Nǎinai said. "The longer it cooks, the better it tastes." We sat in the kitchen, listening to the bubbling water. She sipped tea slowly, as though waiting for something more than the food.

To Māma, who folds the past into every meal.

When I sit with you now, I wonder if you think of Nǎinai when you fold the zongzi. Do you hear her voice in the crackle of bamboo leaves? Do you see her hands in yours as you twist the twine? You don't speak much of the past. But I see it in the way your eyes linger on the stove, in the way you wait for the steam to rise, as if it might carry something lost back to you.

You, Māma, who never learned from Nǎinai because war pulled you too far apart. You learned from neighbors, books, and grainy videos on your phone. You, who had no stories passed down, create them instead. In this kitchen, every fold, every knot, becomes a stitch in the fabric of our family.

When I fumble, you guide me. You never scold—only adjust my hands. "This is how we make sure we don't forget," you say. "This is how we survive."

When I ask what you mean, you only smile, your hands still moving. Wrapping rice and pork, history and heartache, back into the safety of leaves.

When the Ocean Sings

by Lucia Lucchi

The sky bleeds
        into the sea,
swirls of grays and blues,
salt and pepper shakers,
        spilled,
                cluttered,
                        smashed
like the cracked shells
crunching beneath my feet dampened
        by the ocean's graceful touch
full of the truth she leaks like rivers
        through the grainy sand.

The wind is never my friend
when she batters my cheeks
        and turns them pale pink
like the flowy petals
        of a half-burst water lily—
unforgiving as she relays every message the sky has to send
through flurries that melt mid-air
        and swirling cold fronts,
                unseen and unknown
until my entire body is frozen
and the sand turns solid as if in an eye-rolled apology
        for snapping and biting as my heels
like a wild dog.

If the sky and the sea
were to touch beyond the horizon,
        to melt into each other
                so effortlessly
their skins were the same shade,
I would let myself fall
until there's nothing to carry me
        but the breeze of my own breath,
an unreliable source that could s t u t t e r
        and *break*
at any moment when my body decides
        to fail.

To be flying free
        is to be lost in a maze
of tsunamis and currents
        tugging and crushing.
When the ocean sings,
it is like a calling—
        a calling towards home.
Maybe I belong beneath the waves
        or maybe on her frothy shores.
No matter the reason of my journey homeward
        I'll let the ocean calm me,
drain me of my worries.

Of all the things I have learned,
the thing I keep closest
        is that it's a good day
when the ocean sings.

Guardian Angels

by Anna (Adam) Maioli

You turn your eyes to the ones you seeked for help. They left your aid and caused you pain, the guardian angels of the north, west, east, and south, heard the wails of your silent voice. They raise their giant wings of words. They swing down and help you clear the rubble, tend to your burned, crisped wounds, rebuild your home with the green leaves and restore your memories. Do not fear as the angels shed their golden tears, singing their holy words to the angels in the sky. They wrap their wings shielding you. They will help you clear the rubble and rebuild your home and restore your memories.

Roots

by June Oh

Ask me to braid French and my fingers will weave their own clumsy, spontaneous sonata foreign and delightful. Something's not quite right about my knuckles clashing, wrists spiraling in ways they shouldn't spiral, and the stubbornness of these hereditary hands seem more of a burden than a blessing. Even Umma agrees with me in her own manner, clicking her tongue and dispensing weighty sighs as her own fingers try to mimic the grace of the video tutorial.

I let her weave her frustration into my locks, knuckles fading white with each tug and twist, each strand of hair that finds itself at my feet when the torment becomes too much. I count these strands with the taps of my feet—one tap for one strand, two taps for two, all the way until my shins resort to numbness in self-preservation.

My knuckles feel nothing.

I swallow the red that seeps into my tongue to make room for more. Organic means nothing if it doesn't do the work; organic shampoo, organic detangler, organic hairbrush, organic water— and my hair refuses to bend in the prison of Umma's hands.

Your hair isn't meant for this. Umma clicks her tongue, again.

She never finished those braids.

I don't have the heart to tell her that Halmeoni could have tamed the *organic* from these locks with a spell only she knows how to cast, a magic I can only describe as a balletic routine of nimble fingers—*over and under, in and out*—and the fortitude of my hair dissolves within her choreography; a struggle of sixty minutes diminished to twelve. Umma has no words.

Practice means nothing

but not always. Umma's hands still forget to hold, to cross over not under, to have patience, but her tugging has eased and her bitter exhales have lost their consistency. Somehow, Halmeoni seems to have transferred fragments of her magic into Umma's hands when they collided, a connection melting skin-on-skin as Halmeoni's wrinkles embrace Umma's youth. Their fingers fly in sync as my hair sections into halves, halves into quarters, and quarters into eighths, to create the final product of two handsome braids, woven French

Indifferent and unequal

The city of Angels

by Aimee Preciado

Past the untouched snow
of the canyons
the moon rose over the city

The city covered
in the smog
that ages the trees
making them blind
to the true wonders of the world

into the California drought
where the smog
envelopes the city whole
and makes it difficult
for young children to breathe
once vivacious,
lays cold
and still.

i allow the California air
to smother me whole on a
cold, January night
where the air seems to mimic my youth

ashes fall on our heads
on a Thursday afternoon
because we inherited what the fires left.

This World Always and Never Ends

by Seohyun Ryu

—"it's blue." We scream at the top of our
eyes. Our eyes are blind and bold from
the red traffic light. The traffic light turns
green. My umma sees these lights as blue.
Her seasoned spinach is blue. But from
her eyes, they're the color of umma's
umma. My grandma is purple. *i turn the
volume up.* But for my umma she is red.
Red flowers. Like rmaskdghk[1] or Bleeding
Hearts. At this point on the road, i can't
feel the difference between tears and
sweat. They are both liquid. Sticky and
wet. i open the window to freeze the water
and time. The wind glides in between
my fingers and brings back something
i've forgotten. "Rhr ehfdkdhfrp[2]." i don't
want to go back. My umma got mad at
me this morning for never looking ahead.
The "future." i don't like thinking of the "future."
Because there is no future after death. *The
music is too loud.* She doesn't believe i
can die. In her lifetime i never die. If
i didn't see the red traffic light flickering to

[1] "금낭화" typed on an English keyboard
[2] "꼭 돌아올게" typed on an English keyboard

the color blue, did it ever turn blue? At least
in the world i live in, it never turns blue. *i can't
hear anything.* It never turned blue. The song
comes to an end. And i see a speck of light
in the sky. It might just be a satellite, but i
want it to be a star. The satellite turns into
a star. As i beg for this world to never end,
i pluck the star out and tattoo it onto
my ears. But my prayers answer me back
with ends and beginnings. It always and
never ends. Should i cross out "Always" or
"Never"? Does it even matter? The star
explodes in my ears. It rings. The car stops.
We are now 2 minutes and 57 seconds
closer from the sun consuming our
future and "future." But i sold my world
for this very moment. So who cares? i
replay the song. This world—

phase one (point five)

by Ember Tomlinson

---

after Phase One by Dilruba Ahmed

For slipping your shoes on tied and
wearing away at the heel of the sneaker
tucked against your socked foot,
I forgive you.

I forgive you for your bleeding nails after
you have picked the skin around them raw.
I forgive you for the forgotten birthdays
and hastily-wrapped presents.

I forgive you for the stained and torn pages
of the book that you promised you would return.
For leaving your bus pass under your seat,
for your tears.

Fleeing when you were needed most,
your scratchy voice squeaking an apology.
For the way your eyes looked slightly to the
left edge of the floorboards when you lied.

I forgive you for the overdue bills piled on
the kitchen counter and your grumbled dismissal
when I ask you to pull up a chair so we can
try a new blueberry pancake recipe.

For the late nights spent watching Youtube videos
when I have to drag you away from your
"cheese rolling competitions" to ask if
you've drank water yet today.

For the times you rambled too long about
the different joints in a bird's wing
to extended family members whose eyes
glossed over within the first five minutes.

I forgive you for what you cannot change about yourself,
for the half-used toothpaste tubes in the trash
when you swear you can't use any more,
for the wilting leaves of the plant in your

bedroom that you got as a parting gift from
your grandma. For the acne that dapples your
cheeks from shoving your face into all your blankets
to memorize their smell.

For ruining your teeth with soft sodas
and splurging your money on lost lip glosses.
For your unintelligible notes covered in
doodles and scratches in the class that's

professor that always has a story to tell.
For your refusal to buy new shoes because
the white converse ripped at the seam are
those that you've had since your last breakup.

I forgive you for the winter mittens lost in
the clutter of your room, for your short
temper when someone does something wrong, or
when you do something wrong and refuse to admit it.

I forgive you for ordering wedding cards
for your sister with the wrong shade of green,

I forgive you for startling the cats you've
had for years. I forgive you with my

hands and heart that can, with my
tears that fall on your shoulder and arms
that wrap your sorrows tight in a bundle.
I forgive you for the way you refuse to be forgiven.

Line and Dot

by Sofia Travaglino

A line and a dot, when wielded correctly,
can slice a heart in half, thirds, or unevenly.
But if the two like being far away,
they can still cause head- or heart-aches.

The line will never make a shape,
but it doesn't care nor want to at all.
The line can damage without drawing "attention,"
while a shape will make a wound or scar.

A dot, though smaller than a golf ball,
can smash through walls or any skull.
Though it doesn't get blamed for that,
for it has something else attack instead.

Together, they're a powerful weapon.
No blade, but they can cut deep into your heart.
No changes to your brain's shape,
but they still change the way you think.

All you need are a few words,
and you already made your own line.
End the thought with a period,
and now you wield a line and dot.

Wield them carefully, they can cause
stronger damage than you think.

They can even change your own mind,
so use this weapon responsibly.

If you now wield
a line and dot of your own,
then I've wielded mine successfully,
meaning we both win this battle.

"Hope" is the thing with claws

by Mathilda Turich

After "'Hope' is the thing with feathers" by Emily Dickenson

"Hope" is the thing with Claws -
That scratches, swipes, and bites -
Paces the den deep in your Heart -
Sleeps in your bed at night --

Through hailstorms follows - close behind -
And Growls at the wind -
When it bares teeth at ice unkind -
It also clearly Grins --

It pads Sure where you sink in sand -
And grips to scale a spruce -
And when it's trapped by reaching hands -
Reminds you of its use.

A Night in My Life

by Ash Wang

I'm walking around my neighborhood and feeling weightless. I am listening to the gentle crunch of smushed grass blades and dry leaves through the soles of my shoes. Winter in California is not so much felt, it's seen. The few trees that are not evergreen drop their leaves into dusty piles and go barren. My eczema knuckles go dry and crackly like the desert soil. The clouds in the sky seem to absorb sound and everything goes quiet outside and inside. The full moon peeks out of the clouds so bright that it looks like the sun. I go back to my house.

My mom is on the sofa switching through cable channels when I come inside. On the kitchen table is a mandarin orange set on a napkin that she peeled for me. I eat the orange on the sofa, sitting at the crack between the two cushions. She tells me what I missed in the twenty minutes of me being outside and I tell her what she missed when she was inside. I speak without thinking and pet the sleeping dog that is snuggled up to my mom. I'm tired too. The cold tones of news anchor chatter come up and down in waves, the sound lapping at my ankles as I make my way upstairs.

I sit on my special ordered red toilet seat cover making eye contact with the owls on my shower curtain. In elementary school the teachers would tell us to put on our thinking caps. My toilet is my equivalent of a thinking cap. Tonight I'm thinking about how I could roll my body over every tabletop, corner, and crevice of this house. I don't walk through these walls imagining how I look from the perspective of God. I just exist. I brush my teeth, walk through the hallway, peek into the rooms of my dad and sister, and say goodnight. I go to my room.

My favorite stuffed animal, Poohby, is tucked under my pink comforter. My mom made my bed. I slip inside the covers and cradle Poohby in my arms. Poohby is very old in stuffed animal years, 17 years old. Same age as me. When I hug Poohby, I think about all of the nights before this one. So many nights of laying in this bed and rubbing the silk trim at the end of Poohby's dress in between my fingers. In middle school, long hair sprouting from a side part would fan out on my pillow and cover Poohby's nose. In elementary school, Poohby would be whisked to my mom's room in the middle of the night when I had a bad dream. In the cradle, barely conscious, my cries would be silenced by the comfort of Poohby. I am conscious and hugging Poohby, feeling at home. I turn to my side. I'm a side sleeper. Right at my bedside is my notebook. It's full of sad poems about growing up. I like to write about how I feel. What I feel right now is a kind of acceptance. These material things, my home, and my solid body are all made to be destroyed. But right now I am in my body. I'm feeling gravity and the softness of Poohby inside the covers of my bed. I'm not sure how to explain it in words. There are only the facts of the night and the hope that in between the words that are fleeting and forgetful, there is or once was life.

light and alive

by Lily Werve

---

sometimes the dark looks back
peers at you, like a curious stargazer, examining
your face
your shape
your light
it looms over you
a towering redwood
trunk made of lead and leaves of charcoal
who's to say if it thinks
who's to say what it thinks
if it hears your call and response of yelps and giggles
if it giggles back
if it knows things too horrifying that we've drowned them in shadows
the waking world has forgotten how to see
if it is afraid of you too
with your clanging water bottles and thoughts of the stars
if it fears your flashlights and fire and tinsel hair and aluminum skin
and nails of pearls
all echoing with light and
alive
alive
alive
if it sees your glow
if it wishes to glow as you do

Danger's Embrace

by Lyila Wirth

That ancient wine-red door frame
was my finish line ribbon.
Your taut voice that slipped scruff lips
was my starting horn.
I apologized to hundred-meter lightning bolt
stolen seventeen years after.
I've become the child of singer Patsy Cline
walking out after midnight.
That junk yard arrested, 2010 Saturn
was my annex of the hour.
But even the arms that it cradled me in
couldn't protect from bull's eyes.
I was shaking as if dunked in titanic water
when your iceberg crashed.
The man in the moon witnessed every move
my one small step missed.
I thought your hands were to be like a claw machine
but you're more the cheap prize
Tripped off your tongue, to you I'm "brainwashed"
but your mind is what needs cleaned.
You strut back inside, but this isn't fashion week
I sigh, then call for Dad to pick me up.
This is what I'd have to call a danger's embrace
looped like Pop Smoke on Spotify.
Every other weekend, similar stories like tonight
never brought to daylight.

scraps from what has disappeared

by Lucy Yao

There aren't many red doors in the city. Or in beachside suburbias—where the sun's white matches the painted pillars. I imagine it's one of those things that's hard to find, but easy to spot, as you waited for me there. Ice cream dripped down your sleeve and I was waiting for nothing to happen.

For the dogs to bark as I wallowed after. For the clouds to overtake us, a wedding veil hiding us from the orange heat. You were telling me about your future — how you've escaped this crisp downtown with the sandiest air where palm trees serve as palisades. I remember saying *good, I'm happy*. But as the end nears the beginning, as the future becomes the past — this is a moment we are realizing our lives will be changed.

We talked about the last moment like this: college, when I left our villas bordering forest and sea. I remember telling you *I think this is a tale of cycles*, where somehow years later, I am back at the same heartache, at that red door by the shore. I hesitated to call it a wavelength though, because we are not reaching the same peaks every time. We are not pushing and pulling with the moon's tides that remain, relenting, every beach we are near; there's something here in the shape of boomboxes and clay strokes, each resonating in a new shape. We will always miss this street, this house, but a different piece of our hearts have been suckled out; as I'm reminded of blind mothers cradling their baby's leg, feeling each dip and form of bone. I wonder if that has been what's happened here—we are engraved with different words we must feel with each nerve to know its meaning. Mine has said that my heart is always in one timeline as home: this is a story about remembering before things have happened, and crying after we tumble in the dunes.

You told me then that *somehow we have all been chosen for this*, to have our paths cross like the winds intertwine midst a cyclone. I lick ice cream up my arm, as I am sharing and will share smiles with the sun for the present and next time.

But there is no door left today, a week after everything happened. There was an infection that left behind char ink, crumbling with the slightest blow. I was here, and You were at the other shore when our hearts hit the same trough. There is no streets, no houses, no red any-more. The metal frame stands lone against the razed—I imagine a white flag burned away from its mast.

Sooted paint flakes beneath my fingerprints, and I remember this is how dry tears fall as well. How your face must have wrinkled down when you realized what was being lost. How we had never called this place home before, for we thought home was grander, larger, more permanent than this. But how was I supposed to know that I'd only recognize my daydream when it turned into nostalgia. And how was I supposed to tell you then—our voices suspended between telephone lines—even now, we still live there.

Walking

by Alan Yue

Here I am, climbing up a hill and thinking about
how much I love you, that my talent lies elsewhere
and still here I am reaching, slipping, and sitting on wet stones.
That mountain on the other side, where stands a single red
tree left from autumn. I say LORD give me strength
only to stay still and listen to the river.

Here I am, alone, on a mountain that's
so much larger amidst the green. How the trees here hide
the rainwater longer, under layers of dead leaves and looser dirt.
There is a jagged outcropping of rocks—where the hill smooths.
Amidst trees and dry soil I am praying to God for strength
when I collapse. There is a river somewhere, and where
no longer matters.

This hill is so quiet. I yell for someone and seconds later half a voice
tells me *come.*

I keep screaming I LOVE YOU in my head, and then nothing
happens. I yell and
yell and there is only a river now, far away. All I have is a little blood
sludging where I think
my heart should be, right in the center of my chest, and a little air to
breathe

home is a hope

by ariel zhang

---

on six wheels. if you let it
pass through you, it will
linger by your frame, as if
you are a doorway of light.
you can be a doorway to light

Editor

Chiwan Choi is the author of five books of poetry: *The Flood*, the Daughter trilogy—*Abductions*, *The Yellow House* and *my name is wolf*—and *Sky Songs*. He is also Editor at Cultural Daily and part of the experimental literary laboratory, Writ Large Projects.

Cover Artist

Jen Hernandez (she/they) is an artist and educator based in the Pacific Northwest. Her painting, illustration and storytelling in comics centers on themes of nature, adventure, and fantasy inspired by temperate rainforests and Filipino folklore. Her artwork and writing can be found at jenhernandezart.com

Book Designer

J.W. Donley—HWA and HOWL Society member—lives in the Pacific Northwest where the Cascade Mountains meet the Salish Sea. J.W. specializes in editing and formatting horror and other dark fiction and is the author of the novelette *Cats of the Pacific Northwest* and *100 Unusual Prompts for Writers of Horror, Weird, and Bizarro Fiction*. His short stories have appeared in anthologies from Dim Shores, HOWL Society Press, PIT, Chuckanut Editions, and on Creepy, a Horror Podcast.

Contributors

Aimee Preciado

Aimee Preciado is a student at California State University, Bakersfield and writer from McFarland, California. She writes about the profound impact of love lost and life lived. Aimee is a member of The 309 Collective, a group of young California poets, writers, musicians, and artists.

Alan Yue

Alan Yue is a Californian high schooler who learns melodies by ear. He used to eat figs, but now writes free verse. He enjoys experiencing crowds and ostinatos.

Anna Maioli

Anna Maioli, known to some people as Adam, has quite the obsession with questioning the things around her, whether it's her religious beliefs, life, death, political views, or just the dusty old billboard that has been around for 15 years. Having a fascination with African, Latin American, and Iranian cultures, her work mostly goes off the views of countless gods that control her very mind inspired by many gods from many cultures. Pieces of her personality dropped onto a paper writing themselves.

Annie Bryant

Annie Bryant is a seventeen-year-old from a rural town in California. She enjoys soccer, environmental science, reading, and boba tea. Her aspirations include living in a big city, traveling the world, and publishing a book someday.

Ariel Zhang

Ariel is a student from California. She is fond of words, bagels, and sunsets.

Ash Wang

Ash Wang is a writer and artist from Irvine, California, now a first-year student at Fordham University Lincoln Center. Ash is a member of The 309 Collective, a group of young California poets, writers, musicians, and artists.

Basil Lee

Basil Lee is a student at Pittsburgh CAPA (class of 2026). They have received Gold Keys in the Scholastic Art & Writing Awards for journalism and dramatic writing.

Bella Giammalvo

Bella Giammalvo is a Los Angeles-based student writer. She's fond of pretty trinkets, the ocean at night, and lots of Lana Del Rey. Her writing illuminates the clash where future meets present, in an attempt to understand the struggle between support and intervention, self and other, and love and loss. Bella is a member of The 309 Collective, a group of young California poets, writers, musicians, and artists.

Chloe Crawford

My name is Chloe Crawford, and I am a junior at Pittsburgh CAPA. I major in creative writing, and I really enjoy writing poetry.

Ember Tomlinson

Ember Tomlinson's favorite word, pneumonoultramicroscopicsilicovolcanoconiosis, is 45 letters long. Previously, they have won a city-wide Do The Write Thing award and a Silver Key in the Scholastic Art and Writing Awards. They always have an array of random facts on hand, ready to turn anything into inspiration for their next piece. Ember is passionate about physics and astronomy and has a variety of interests across multiple fields. Writing makes them feel free, like they can float as far as they want with their only companion being the humming of a stream and vibrant words.

Emily Liu

Emily Liu, a poet and writer from the San Francisco Bay Area, navigates the liminal spaces of memory, loss, and transformation. In her free time, she enjoys curating Spotify playlists and exploring the city with friends in search of the best boba spots.

Hana Lang

Hana Lang is currently a highschooler at CAPA 6-12. She was born and raised in Pittsburgh PA. Hana recently won a Scholastic Silver Key and has won the Better Together Essay contest. Hana enjoys sailing a flying junior, playing music, and spending time in art museums. Her favorite genres of writing are poetry and playwriting. Her influences are her brother, Alexander Pope, Malcolm Todd, and Jazz.

Honor Giardini

Honor Giardini is a student and writer from rural northern California. Her poems and essays have been published in Roxane Gay's Emerging Writer Series, Orca Literary Journal, and Cultural Daily. She is the recipient of the Herb Alpert Award for Emerging Young Artists. Honor is a 2024 Foyle Young Poet and a 2025 National YoungArts winner with distinction. She is an alumnus of Iowa Young Writers Studio and California State Summer School for the Arts.

Jiyoo Kim-Jung

Jiyoo Kim-Jung is a high school student from the United States who writes poetry and short stories in order to explore her inner thoughts. She has been writing stories for around nine years and has been writing poetry for a little over one. In her free time, she can be found playing the piano and drafting poems about playing the piano.

Joshua Granados

Joshua Granados is a high school junior born and raised in Los Angeles, California. When he is not playing football and lacrosse, he enjoys drumming and spending time with his friends. He recently graduated from phase 1 of the LAFD/Paramedic cadet program, and he is passionate about helping others, especially through social justice.

June Oh

June Oh is a poet and screenwriter from Los Angeles, California. Her work has been recognized by Cultural Daily, Cherry Blue, Bitter Melon Review, and LA Student Film Awards, among others. In her free time, she volunteers at dog rescues and enjoys dancing like nobody's watching.

Leah An

Leah An is a freshman in high school. She lives in San Diego and enjoys writing and reading. In her free time, Leah likes to have coffee dates with her mom and sister.

Lila Coen

Lila Coen is a poet from Madison, Wisconsin. She loves writing and is a two time CSSSA alumni. When she is not writing, you can find her seeing her friends, playing with her dog, or listening to music.

Lilia Werve

Lily Werve is a high school senior at Calabasas High School and a Scholastic Gold Medal winning writer. As a native Angeleno, she has been evacuated due to the Woolsey Fire (2018) and the Palisades Fire (2025). She is so grateful for the opportunity to contribute to this volume.

Lucia Lucchi

Lucia Lucchi was born and raised in Squirrel Hill, a neighborhood in Pittsburgh, PA. She is currently a high-schooler at CAPA 6-12. She is a Virgo and has two sisters, a dog, a bunny, and three betta fish. Her favorite comfort food is mac & cheese and she loves anything chocolate, sweet, and cheesy. In her free time, she enjoys rock climbing and crafting.

Lucy Yao

Lucy Yao is a freshman at Northwestern University, and raised in California. She is attached to images and poignant irony of them. Each symbol leads to another, and another, and another, which often becomes the very centerpiece of her poetry. When she's not writing, she's talking, whether to read out her own slam poetry, interview for her journalistic and club endeavors, or to go on tangents about her unfunded fashion and entertainment needs.

Lyila Wirth

Lyila Wirth (aka Lanni because her friends think she is incredibly nonchalant and needed a better nickname than nonchalanty) is from a small farm town in Central PA called Mifflinburg where horses and buggies rule the rural roads. Lyila has been writing since age seven, first making comics about pieces of toast, who save their toaster planet day after day. To date, she has expanded her writing to poetry, song-writing, short stories, fiction and nonfiction.

Mathilda Turich

Mathilda Turich is a 12th Grade Literary Artist at Pittsburgh CAPA, an activist, and a farmer. She likes strange poetry, native plants, and long walks in the stream. Yesterday she lost a shoe in a mucky pond. His passion for nature—and how it's not so separate from human-ity—inspires much of his writing. In their free time they're an avid gardener, musician, and martial artist.

Michelle Bi

Michelle Bi is a writer from Oak Park, CA. She is currently in her first year of study at Brown University. In her free time she enjoys making far too many Spotify playlists, taking pictures of trees, and attempting to perfect her earl grey tea recipe.

Milla Jans

Milla Jans is a writer from Southern California, and she spends much of her time writing pieces exploring life from various perspectives. In the future, she hopes to publish a book of poetry and photography,

Miriam Davison

Miriam Davison is a writer and high school senior from Los Angeles, CA. She is an alumnus of the Iowa Young Writers' Studio and has been recognized by the Scholastic Awards for her writing. Next year, she will enroll at Brown University '29, where she will continue to write and drink coffee past noon.

Navya Chitlur

Navya Chitlur is a teen poet from the Bay Area who writes to make sense of pasts and emotions. She lives and dies for gothic and dark literature, indie and pop albums, and art deco aesthetics. She also loves baking and water sports.

Pippa Barlow

Pippa Barlow is a ninth-grade literary arts student at CAPA. She recently won a Scholastic Gold Key for her poem "I Hate Poetry." She started writing at two years old when she dictated picture books such as Doctor Horse to her mother. Since then, she has started many and finished few writing projects. Pippa lives in Pittsburgh, PA with her parents and younger brother, though in her heart she lives in a castle in Scotland.

Rasheedat Ibrahim

Rasheedat Ibrahim is a seventeen-year-old 11th grader at Pittsburgh CAPA. She was born on January 6th, 2008. She loves staying active, a lot of her best memories with the outdoors. She loves all things sports and the summertime. She loves to connect her physical experiences with her abstract writing style. She hopes to be a gym teacher or work in finance someday.

Semi Jung

Semi Jung is a 17-year-old South Korean writer based in the Bay Area. She writes poetry, fiction, and very messy pieces that are a blend of the two.

Seohyun Ryu

What is the earliest form of memory you hold? Seohyun Ryu is a California Arts Scholar who writes to make a moment breathe on a page forever like a scar. Because what's more beautiful than the coexistence of life and death? Every faded memory is a catalyst for a new story.

Read more of Seohyun's scars at Outlander Zine, Orangepeel Literary Magazine, Decolonization Dialogue, Cultural Daily, and more.

Shyla Corona

A Hispanic creative who writes with the goal of creating change in her community. As an LA native, she spends her time exploring coffee shops and bookstores while looking for inspiration. When returning home from her adventures, she enjoys reading, crocheting, and learning new things. Her love of history and the intricacies of human connection are often featured in her works.

Sofia Travaglino

My name is Sofia Travaglino, I am a literary artist at Pittsburgh CAPA. My poems are primarily based on my own feelings, experiences, and whatever is on my mind. Though I have never visited California, my father lived in Los Angeles for a lot of his career. A lot of his friends have been affected by the wildfires, which has worried him a lot. I want to help all of those affected by the wildfires, whether directly or indirectly, as much as I can.

www.ingramcontent.com/pod-product-compliance
Lightning Source LLC
Chambersburg PA
CBHW030944310726
48969CB00008B/2379